PLAYING THE CELLO

BOOK ONE

BY CASSIA HARVEY

CHP300

1. Remember the A string

Cassia Harvey

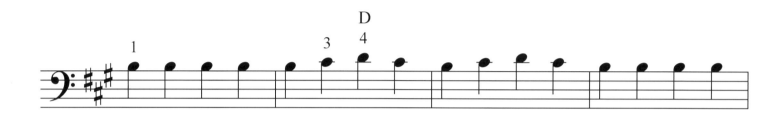

2. Remember the A string with
Mississippi Hot Dog

Mix it up a little!

3. The Double Notes Song

Each note here
gets 2 counts!

4. Remember Mary Had a Little Lamb?

5. Remember the Notes on the D string

6. Practicing and then Playing a D major scale

Memorize the D major scale:

7. Russian Folk Song

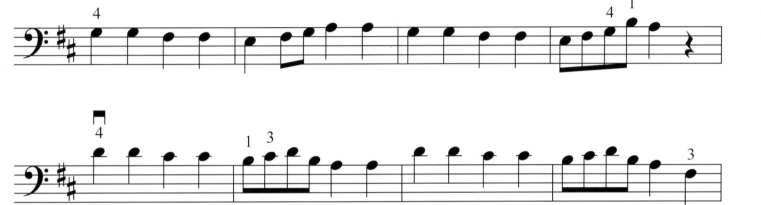

8. Theme from Dvorak's Symphony

Wait while the piano plays
8 measures, then go to the
beginning and repeat.

9. Finger Training on D and A

10. Exercise for 1812

11. Tchaikovsky's 1812 Overture

12. *Spring* from Vivaldi's "Four Seasons"

13. Finger Study

14. Slow Bows: Each note gets 3 counts!

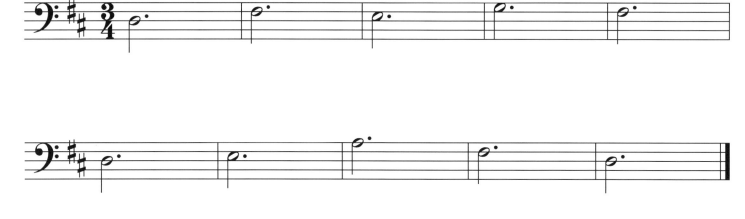

15. Slow Bows: Each note gets 4 counts!

16. *The Carnival of Venice*; a song with rests

17. For He's a Jolly Good Fellow

18. Note Practice while Violins Learn the E string

3rd finger on the C string.

19. Practicing while the Violins play the A Major Scale

20. The Minstrel Boy

21. A Minuet by Bach for Violins and Basses

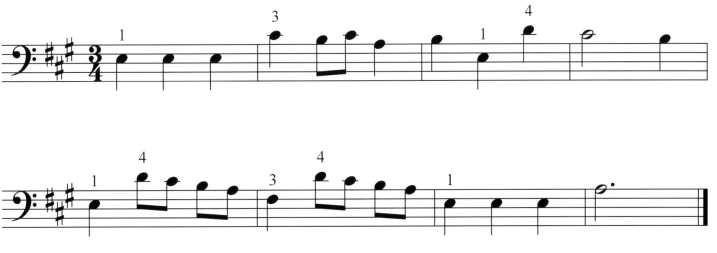

22. The Minstrel Boy for Violas, Cellos, and Basses

23. A Minuet by Bach for Violas and Cellos

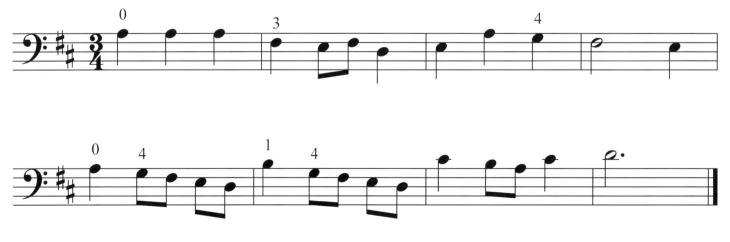

This page left blank to
eliminate page turns.

24. (Violins Learn Fourth Finger)

25. String Crossing Practice for Telemann

26. Telemann Allegro from Solo #7

27. Telemann Allegro from Solo #7 for Violas and Cellos

28. The Skipping Workout

29. Hornpipe

30. Lady George Murray's Reel

31. Exercise with E

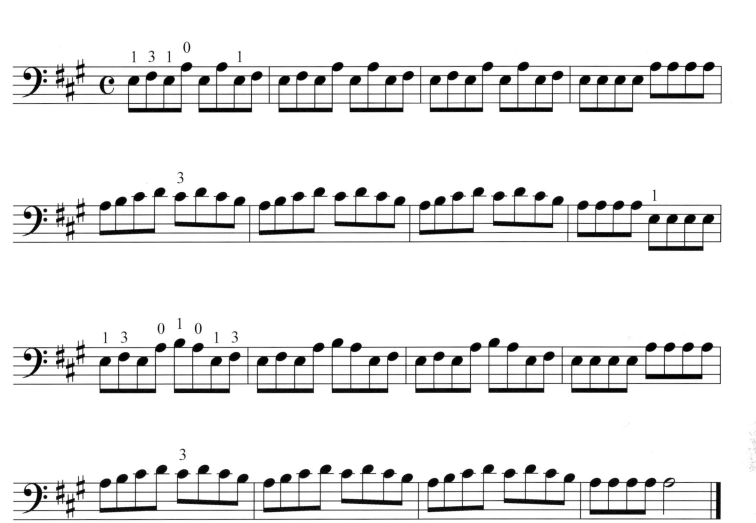

32. Exercise on D

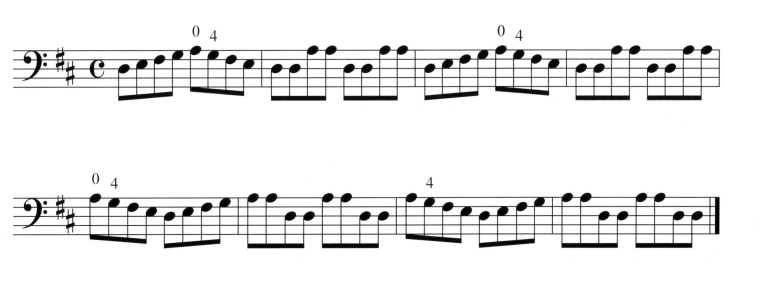

33. Minuet on "Duncan Grey" for Violins and Basses

Advanced Variation for Violins

34. Minuet on "Duncan Grey" for Violas and Cellos

Advanced Variation for Violas, Cellos, Basses

35. Skipping Fingers on D, A, and with E

37. Fiddle Exercise

38. Violins Train on the E String

39. Over the River and Through the Woods

40. Captain Oakus

41. The Notes on the G string

42. A Menuett by Leopold Mozart

43. A Menuett by J. S. Bach

44. British White Feathers Using the G String

45. Rameau's *Tambourin*

46. We Wish You a Merry Christmas

47. Shalom Chaverim

48. Happy Birthday

49. Happy Birthday Variation

This page left blank to
eliminate page turns.

50. Cellos and Violas Work on the C String

51. C Scale Exercise

52. Skye Boat Song

53. Red Red Rose

Arranged Myanna Harvey

Use 2nd finger
here to play
F natural.

54. Such a Parcel of Rogues!

55. The Snake Charmer's Dance for Cellos and Violas

Interlude

56. The Snake Charmer's Dance for Violins and Bass

57. Bonaparte's Retreat

available from **www.charveypublications.com**
The *Getting in Shape* Series

Early-Intermediate Series:
Getting in Shape
In these multi-level string class books, each exercise and short piece is presented first in easy (A) format and then in slightly more difficult (B) format. The less-advanced (A) pages are structured so that they can be played together with more-advanced (B) pages and students of different levels can play together in the same class. These books work with homogeneous or mixed-string classes.

Getting in Shape for Violin **CHP123**
Getting in Shape for Viola **CHP124**
Getting in Shape for Cello **CHP125**
Getting in Shape for Bass **CHP126**

Made in the USA
Coppell, TX
31 March 2020